thai

simple and delicious easy-to-make recipes

Lesley Mackley

This is a Parragon Publishing Book
First published in 2002

Parragon Publishing
Queen Street House
4 Queen Street
Bath BA1 1HE
United Kingdom

ISBN: 1-84273-483-0

Printed in China

Produced by The Bridgewater Book Company Ltd

Creative Director Terry Jeavons
Art Director Sarah Howerd
Editorial Director Fiona Biggs
Senior Editor Mark Truman
Assistant Editor Tom Kitch
Photographer Simon Punter
Home Economist Ricky Turner
Page Make-up Chris and Jane Lanaway
Prop hunter Sarah Allaway

COVER
Photographer Ian Parsons
Home Economist Sara Hesketh

Acknowledgements
The publishers would like to thank the following
for the use of properties: Spoils, Cargo, and Debenhams,
Brighton, UK.

NOTES FOR THE READER

- This book uses both imperial and metric measurements. Follow the same units of measurement throughout; do not mix imperial and metric.
- All spoon measurements are level: teaspoons are assumed to be 5 ml, and tablespoons are assumed to be 15 ml.
- Unless otherwise stated, milk is assumed to be whole, eggs and individual vegetables such as potatoes are medium, and pepper is freshly ground black pepper.
- Recipes using raw or very lightly cooked eggs should be avoided by infants, the elderly, pregnant women, convalescents, and anyone suffering from an illness.
- Optional ingredients, variations, or serving suggestions have not been included in the calculations. The times given are an approximate guide only. Preparation times differ according to the techniques used by different people and the cooking times may also vary.

contents

introduction

Thai cooking has become increasingly popular in the last few years, and the main ingredients, which not so long ago could be found only in specialist shops, have now become widely available.

Chiles are an essential ingredient in many dishes, and if you are not used to them, add them with caution. However, the use of coconut milk and fragrant herbs and spices has a cooling effect on the heat of the chiles. It should not be difficult to find the other ingredients used in these recipes, but if, for instance, fresh lemongrass or lime leaves are unavailable, it will not affect the recipe if dried ones are used. Lemongrass is also available in a purée. If you find fresh lime leaves and lemongrass, it is worth stocking up, because they freeze very well. Fish sauce is the Thai equivalent to soy sauce and is used as a seasoning instead of salt. It gives a distinctive flavor to many Thai dishes, but if it is difficult to find, use soy sauce instead.

Many dishes in this book are suitable for vegetarians, and you can substitute soy sauce for fish sauce when the latter occurs in an otherwise vegetarian recipe. Thai cooking can be addictive, and once you are familiar with the ingredients and able to balance different flavors, you will enjoy adapting the recipes to your own taste.

guide to recipe key		
	easy	Recipes are graded as follows: 1 pea = easy; 2 peas = very easy; 3 peas = extremely easy.
	serves 4	Recipes generally serve four people. Simply halve the ingredients to serve two, taking care not to mix imperial and metric measurements.
	10 minutes	Preparation time. Where marinating or soaking noodles are involved, these times have been added on separately: eg, 15 minutes + 30 minutes to marinate.
	10 minutes	Cooking time.

hot chile relish with crudités
page 20

shrimp & pineapple curry
page 28

peanut crusted chicken with dipping sauce
page 56

thai bananas
page 90

soups, appetizers & snacks

In Thailand, soups usually stay on the table throughout the meal. They can serve as a sauce for rice or dishes that have no sauce of their own. Some soups, such as Hot & Sour Fish Soup, are very light and can be served as a first course, whereas others are more substantial and may be served as a light lunch or supper dish. Finger food, particularly when sold on the street, is very popular in Thailand. Snacks such as Spring Rolls, Chicken Satay, or Hot Chile Relish with Crudités (Nam Prik) can be served as an appetizer or as party food with drinks.

chicken & coconut milk soup

extremely easy	
serves 4	
10 minutes	
15 minutes	

ingredients

1¾ cups canned coconut milk
scant 2¼ cups chicken bouillon
6 thin slices fresh galangal
2 stalks fresh lemongrass, bruised
4 fresh kaffir lime leaves
8 oz/225 g chicken breast fillets,
   cut into strips

2 red chiles, seeded and
   sliced finely
4 scallions, sliced finely
4 tbsp fish sauce
2 tbsp lime juice
2 tbsp chopped fresh cilantro

Place the coconut milk, chicken bouillon, galangal, lemongrass and lime leaves in a large pan and bring to a boil.

Add the chicken, then reduce the heat and simmer, uncovered, for 10 minutes, or until the chicken is cooked.

Add the chiles and scallions and simmer for 3 more minutes.

Stir in the fish sauce, lime juice, and cilantro and serve immediately, in warmed bowls.

hot & sour
shrimp soup

		ingredients	
very easy	1 lb 2 oz/500 g large raw shrimp, in shells	BOUILLON
		1 lb/450 g white fish bones
serves 4–6	1 cup oyster mushrooms, sliced thinly	8 cups water
		2 stalks of fresh lemongrass, chopped finely
	2 tsp light soy sauce	
	1 tsp white sugar	2–4 small dried red chilis
30 minutes	4 scallions, sliced finely	4 fresh or dried kaffir lime leaves
	2 tsp fish sauce	1 inch/2.5 cm fresh root ginger, peeled
	2 tbsp chopped fresh cilantro	
30 minutes		2 slices of fresh or dried galangal

To make the bouillon, shell the shrimp and place the shells in a large pan with the fish bones, water, lemongrass, chilis, lime leaves, ginger, and galangal. Bring to a boil, then reduce the heat and simmer, covered for 20 minutes.

Strain the bouillon into another large pan. Add the shrimp, mushrooms, soy sauce, sugar, and scallions. Bring back to a boil, then reduce the heat and simmer for 3 minutes, or until the shrimp are cooked. Add the fish sauce and cilantro, then cook for 1 more minute. Serve immediately.

aromatic chicken
& vegetable soup

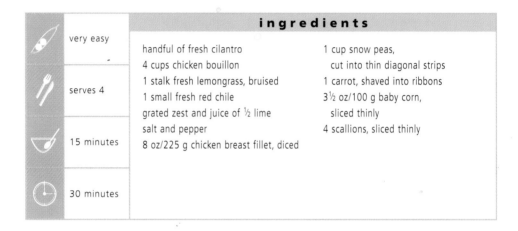

very easy	
serves 4	
15 minutes	
30 minutes	

ingredients

handful of fresh cilantro
4 cups chicken bouillon
1 stalk fresh lemongrass, bruised
1 small fresh red chile
grated zest and juice of ½ lime
salt and pepper
8 oz/225 g chicken breast fillet, diced

1 cup snow peas,
  cut into thin diagonal strips
1 carrot, shaved into ribbons
3½ oz/100 g baby corn,
  sliced thinly
4 scallions, sliced thinly

Strip the cilantro leaves from the stalks. Reserve the leaves and place the stalks in a large pan with the bouillon, lemongrass, chile and lime zest. Bring to a boil, then reduce the heat and simmer, covered, for 15 minutes.

Strain the bouillon into another pan. Add the lime juice, and salt and pepper to taste.

Add the chicken to the bouillon. Bring to a boil, then reduce the heat and simmer for 5 minutes. Add the snow peas, carrot and corn and simmer for about 2 minutes, or until the vegetables are tender and the chicken is cooked.

Coarsely chop the cilantro leaves and stir into the soup with the scallions. Serve immediately.

spring rolls

		ingredients	
easy		1 tbsp vegetable oil	1 inch/2.5 cm piece root ginger,
		2¼ cups lean ground pork	grated finely
makes 30		1 garlic clove, crushed	2 tbsp chopped fresh cilantro
		1 red chile, seeded and	2 tsp fish sauce
		chopped finely	30 spring roll wrappers
20 minutes		4 oz/115 g cooked shrimp, shelled,	oil, for deep frying
		and chopped	
		2 scallions, chopped finely	sweet chile sauce, to serve
15 minutes (food cooked in batches)			

Heat the oil in a skillet. Add the pork, garlic and chile and cook, stirring until the pork is browned.

Add the shrimp, scallions, ginger, cilantro and fish sauce. Cook, stirring, until heated through. Remove from the heat and set aside to cool.

Prepare the spring roll wrappers as directed on the packet.

Place a spoonful of the pork mixture down the middle of each spring roll sheet, leaving a space at the top and bottom and down the side. Brush the edges with water. Fold the top and bottom over and then fold in the sides to form a sealed roll.

Just before serving, heat the oil for frying in a large skillet or wok until nearly smoking. Deep-fry the rolls, in batches, for 2–3 minutes, or until golden brown. Drain on paper towels while cooking the remainder. Serve with sweet chili dipping sauce.

chicken satay

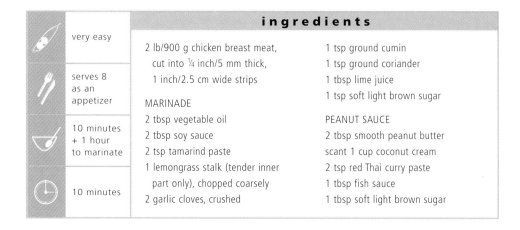

		ingredients	
very easy	2 lb/900 g chicken breast meat, cut into ¼ inch/5 mm thick, 1 inch/2.5 cm wide strips	1 tsp ground cumin 1 tsp ground coriander 1 tbsp lime juice 1 tsp soft light brown sugar	
serves 8 as an appetizer	MARINADE 2 tbsp vegetable oil		
10 minutes + 1 hour to marinate	2 tbsp soy sauce 2 tsp tamarind paste 1 lemongrass stalk (tender inner part only), chopped coarsely 2 garlic cloves, crushed	PEANUT SAUCE 2 tbsp smooth peanut butter scant 1 cup coconut cream 2 tsp red Thai curry paste 1 tbsp fish sauce 1 tbsp soft light brown sugar	
10 minutes			

Thread the chicken onto bamboo skewers.

To make the marinade, place the oil, soy sauce, tamarind paste, lemongrass, garlic, cumin, coriander, lime juice, and sugar in a food processor and blend to make a paste. Transfer to a bowl.

Add the chicken to the marinade and toss to coat. Cover with plastic wrap and refrigerate for at least 1 hour to marinate.

To make the peanut sauce, put the peanut butter, coconut cream, red Thai curry paste, fish sauce, and sugar in a pan. Heat gently, stirring, to form a smooth sauce.

Grill the chicken on a barbecue or under a broiler for 3–5 minutes on each side, or until the chicken is cooked through. Reheat the sauce, adding a little hot water if necessary, and serve with the chicken satays.

thai pork appetizer

		ingredients	
very easy			
serves 6	4 garlic cloves, chopped finely	2 tbsp fish sauce	
	2 fresh red chiles, seeded and	1 tsp soft light brown sugar	
	chopped finely	2 tbsp coarsely chopped fresh cilantro	
	1 tbsp chopped coriander root		
	1 tbsp grated fresh ginger		
20 minutes	3 tbsp vegetable oil	GARNISH	
	1 tbsp hot water	fresh cilantro leaves	
	1 lb 2 oz/500 g lean ground pork	thin strips of red chile	
	2 fresh kaffir lime leaves,		
20 minutes	shredded finely	crisp lettuce cups, to serve	

Place the garlic, chiles, coriander root, ginger, oil and water in a blender, then blend until smooth. Transfer to a wok or skillet.

Heat and stir the paste for 4 minutes over a medium heat, then increase the heat and add the ground pork. Stir-fry for 3 minutes, or until colored.

Add the lime leaves, fish sauce, sugar, and chopped cilantro. Continue to cook, stirring, until the pork is dry.

Serve the pork in lettuce cups, garnished with cilantro leaves and strips of chile.

hot chile relish
with crudités

		ingredients	
extremely easy		**RELISH**	**SERVING SUGGESTIONS**
		8–10 large red chiles, seeded	carrot sticks
serves 4		and chopped finely	radishes
		6 garlic cloves, chopped finely	cucumber batons
10 minutes		½ cup water	baby corn
		½ tsp salt	
		2 tsp sugar	
15 minutes		juice of 1 lime	
		1 tbsp fish sauce	
		1 tbsp vegetable oil	

Put all the relish ingredients in a pan and bring to a boil. Cover and simmer for 10 minutes.

Transfer the relish to a bowl and serve with vegetables.

thai omelet

		ingredients	
✎	very easy	6 eggs salt and pepper 1 tbsp butter 1 tbsp oil	2 tomatoes, peeled, seeded, and cut into ½ inch/1 cm dice 2 tsp fish sauce 1 tsp sugar 2 tsp lime juice
🍴	serves 2		
🥣	15 minutes	FILLING 1 tbsp oil 1 small onion, chopped finely 1 garlic clove, crushed	1 tbsp tomato ketchup 4 scallions, chopped finely
🕐	30–35 minutes	1 cup ground pork 1 cup green peas	salad, to serve

To make the filling, first heat the oil in a skillet. Add the onion and garlic and cook gently for 10 minutes, or until soft. Add the pork and cook, stirring, for 5 minutes, or until colored.

Add the peas, tomatoes, fish sauce, sugar, lime juice, tomato ketchup, and scallions. Cook, stirring, for 10 minutes, adding a little water if the mixture is too dry.

In a bowl, whisk 3 of the eggs and season with salt and pepper.

Heat half the butter and oil in an omelet pan. Add the eggs and cook for 2–3 minutes, pulling in the edges with a fork and letting any egg run to the bottom of the pan.

When almost set, place half the filling mixture on 1 half of the omelet. Fold over and transfer to a plate. Keep warm while making the second omelet. Serve with salad.

fish
& seafood

Thailand has a long coastline and a large number of the people live near the sea. They have always made use of the abundance of fish and shellfish, and Thai cuisine includes many delicious recipes for fish, shrimp, crabs, and mussels. Traditional Thai dishes such as Fish Cakes and Shrimp & Pineapple Curry are quick and easy to make using ready-made Thai fish sauce, while Tiger Shrimp Skewers and Spiced Steamed Fish will liven up any dinner table.

thai fish cakes

		ingredients	
	very easy	1 lb 2 oz/500 g skinless, boneless	SERVING SUGGESTIONS
		cod fillet, cut into chunks	salad
		1 tbsp red curry paste	green beans
	serves 4	1 egg, beaten	broccoli
		1 tsp brown sugar	snow peas
	15 minutes + 30 minutes to chill	1 tsp salt	
		1 tbsp cornstarch	
		½ cup green beans, chopped finely	
		1 tbsp chopped fresh cilantro	
	30 minutes	4 tbsp oil, for frying	
		lime wedges, to garnish	

Put the cod into in a food processor and chop coarsely. Add the curry paste, egg, sugar, salt and cornstarch. Blend well.

Stir in the green beans and cilantro.

Transfer to a bowl and cover with plastic wrap, then chill in the refrigerator for 30 minutes. Roll the mixture into 12 balls, then flatten each ball into a 2 inch/5 cm cake.

Heat the oil in a skillet over a medium heat and cook the cakes in batches for about 3 minutes on each side, or until golden brown and cooked through. Keep the cooked fish cakes warm in a low oven while cooking the remainder.

Garnish with the lime wedges and serve with salad or stir-fried green vegetables such as beans, snow peas, or broccoli.

shrimp & pineapple curry

		ingredients	

extremely easy		2 cups coconut cream
		½ fresh pineapple, peeled
		  and chopped
		2 tbsp Thai red curry paste
		2 tbsp fish sauce
		2 tsp sugar
			12 oz/350 g raw tiger shrimp, shelled
			  and de-veined
			2 tbsp chopped fresh cilantro
			
			4 scallions, shredded, to garnish
			steamed jasmine rice, to serve

serves 4			
10 minutes			
10–15 minutes			

Place the coconut cream, pineapple, curry paste, fish sauce, and sugar in a skillet. Heat gently over a medium heat until almost boiling. Add the shrimp and cilantro and simmer gently for 3 minutes, or until the shrimp are cooked.

Sprinkle with the shredded scallions and serve with steamed jasmine rice.

thai fish curry

		ingredients	
easy	4 shallots, chopped coarsely	½ tsp salt
	2 inch/5 cm fresh root ginger, peeled	1¾ cups coconut cream
serves 4	and sliced finely	4 fish steaks, eg cod, halibut
	2 inch/5 cm fresh lemongrass,	
	outer leaves discarded	GARNISH
	2 inch/5 cm fresh galangal, peeled	1 red chile, cut into thin strips
20 minutes	and chopped finely	2 tbsp toasted slivered almonds
	3 red chiles, seeded and	
	chopped coarsely	TO SERVE
20 minutes	1 tbsp ground almonds	cooked white rice
	½ tsp turmeric	salad

Place the shallots, ginger, lemongrass, galangal, chiles, ground almonds, turmeric, and salt in a blender. Add 6 tablespoons of the coconut cream. Blend to a smooth paste.

Pour the paste into a large skillet. Bring to a boil and cook, stirring, for 4 minutes. Add the remaining coconut milk and bring back to a boil.

Place the fish steaks in the skillet and simmer for 10 minutes, turning once, until the fish is cooked and flakes when tested with a fork. If the sauce is too thin, transfer the fish to a heated serving dish and boil the sauce to reduce to the desired consistency. Garnish with the red chile and toasted almonds and serve with rice and a salad of your choice.

tiger shrimp skewers

	ingredients	
easy	MARINADE	2 tbsp rice wine or dry sherry
	3 garlic cloves, crushed	12 raw tiger shrimp, in shells
serves 4 as an appetizer or 2 as a main dish	2 shallots, chopped finely	
	1 inch/2.5 cm fresh root ginger, peeled and grated finely	GARNISH
		cilantro sprigs
	1 lemongrass stalk, chopped finely	lime wedges
15 minutes + 1 hour to marinate	1 fresh red chile, chopped finely	
	pinch of salt	3 oranges, to serve
	1 tbsp lime juice	
5 minutes	1 tbsp soy sauce	

To make the marinade, place the garlic, shallots, ginger, lemongrass, chile, salt, lime juice, soy sauce, and rice wine or sherry in a blender and blend until smooth. Transfer to a shallow bowl.

Using a small knife, or scissors, split the shrimp shells down the back, but leave attached. De-vein if necessary. Add to the marinade. Cover with plastic wrap and place in the refrigerator to marinate for 30 minutes to 1 hour.

Thread each shrimp onto a bamboo skewer, inserting the skewer at the tail and coming out at the head end until the pointed end extends at least 3 inches/7 cm beyond the shrimp.

Broil for 2 minutes on each side, or until the shrimp are pink and cooked through. Garnish with the cilantro sprigs and lime wedges. Stick the skewers in the orange, to serve.

spiced steamed fish

	ingredients	
very easy	1 inch/2.5 cm piece ginger, grated finely	2 kaffir lime leaves, sliced thinly
	1 lemongrass stalk (base only), sliced thinly	2 sprigs fresh basil leaves
serves 4–6	6 fresh red chiles, seeded and chopped coarsely	TO SERVE
	1 small red onion, chopped finely	cooked rice
10 minutes	1 tbsp fish sauce	cucumber batons
20–25 minutes	2 lb/900 g whole fish (eg sea bass, red snapper, trout, tilapia), cleaned	

Place the ginger, lemongrass, chiles, onion, and fish sauce in a blender. Chop coarsely to a rough paste, adding a little water, if necessary.

Cut 3–4 deep slits crosswise on each side of the fish. Spread over the spice paste, rubbing it well into the slits.

Place the fish in a dish deep enough to hold the liquid that collects during steaming. Sprinkle over the lime leaves and basil.

Set up a steamer or put a rack into a wok or deep skillet. Bring about 2 inches/5 cm of water to a boil in the steamer or wok. Put the dish of fish into the steamer or onto the rack. Reduce the heat to a simmer. Cover tightly and steam the fish for 15–20 minutes, or until the fish is cooked through. Serve with rice and cucumber batons.

fragrant mussels

easy	
serves 2–3 as a main course, 4–6 as an appetizer	
10 minutes	
15–20 minutes	

ingredients

2 lb 4 oz/1 kg mussels, cleaned

2 tbsp water

1 lemongrass stalk, bruised

2 garlic cloves, crushed

3 fresh or dried kaffir lime leaves, chopped coarsely

scant 1 cup coconut cream

2 tbsp chopped fresh cilantro

salt and pepper

warm, crusty bread, to serve

Clean the mussels by scrubbing the shells and pulling out any beards that are attached. Rinse well, discarding any that are broken or remain open when tapped.

Put the water, lemongrass, garlic, and lime leaves in a large pan. Heat until boiling. Add the mussels, then cover and cook for 5–6 minutes, or until they have opened. Discard any that stay closed. Transfer the mussels to a heated serving dish, then cover and keep warm in a low oven.

Boil the cooking liquid hard until reduced by half, then stir in the coconut cream. Boil to reduce and thicken slightly. Add the cilantro and season to taste.

Pour over the mussels and serve with warm, crusty bread.

meat
& poultry

Chicken and duck are widely used in Thai cooking. Many families keep their own chickens and ducks and, because they are free range, they tend to be smaller and tougher than the ones we buy. Most recipes, such as the traditional Green Chicken Curry, are quickly prepared in a wok. Pork is the most popular meat, but beef is also used in classical recipes such as Masaman Beef Curry. Lamb is becoming more popular and, in most of the recipes, the meat used can be varied to suit your taste. Also in this section are main course salads made with beef or duck.

grilled beef salad

		ingredients	
very easy	DRESSING	scant $\frac{2}{3}$ cup dried oyster mushrooms
	2 tbsp sesame oil	1 lb 5 oz/600 g rump steak
serves 4	2 tbsp fish sauce	1 red bell pepper, seeded and
	2 tbsp sweet sherry	sliced thinly
	2 tbsp oyster sauce	generous $\frac{1}{4}$ cup roasted cashew nuts
10 minutes + 20 minutes to soak mushrooms	1 tbsp lime juice	
	1 fresh red chile, seeded and	red and green lettuce leaves, to serve
	chopped finely	mint leaves, to garnish
5–10 minutes		

To make the dressing, place the sesame oil, fish sauce, sherry, oyster sauce, lime juice, and chile in a bowl and whisk to combine.

Place the mushrooms in a bowl, then cover with boiling water and let stand for 20 minutes. Drain and cut into thin slices.

Grill the beef, either on a ridged iron grill pan or under the broiler, turning once, for 5 minutes, or until browned on both sides and rare in the middle, or cook longer if desired.

Slice the steak into thin strips and place in a bowl with the mushrooms, bell pepper, and nuts. Add the dressing and toss together.

Arrange the lettuce on a serving platter and place the beef mixture on top. Garnish with mint and serve at room temperature.

thai beef curry

		ingredients	
easy	3 tbsp vegetable oil	6 cardamom pods, crushed
	1 lb 12 oz/800 g braising steak, cubed	1 small pineapple, peeled
serves 4	2 onions, sliced thinly	and chopped
	2 tbsp Thai red curry paste	
	1 tbsp tamarind paste or lime juice	TO SERVE
	2 tbsp fish sauce	cooked rice
15 minutes	3¾ cups coconut milk	shrimp chips
	2 tsp sugar	
1½–2 hours		

Heat the oil in a flameproof casserole. Brown the beef in batches and set aside.

Add the onions to the oil and cook for 5 minutes, then set aside with the beef. Add the curry paste and cook gently for 1 minute, stirring constantly.

Stir in the tamarind paste, the fish sauce, coconut milk, and sugar. Bring to a boil, then reduce the heat and return the beef and onions to the casserole with the cardamom.

Simmer gently, uncovered, for 1–1½ hours, or until the meat is tender. Stir from time to time and if it is becoming dry, cover with a lid.

Add the pineapple and cook for 5 more minutes. The curry should be quite dry, but add a little water if necessary.

Serve with rice and shrimp chips.

pork steaks
with lemongrass

		ingredients	
extremely easy		MARINADE 2 garlic cloves, crushed ½ tsp freshly ground black pepper 1 tbsp sugar 2 tbsp fish sauce	4 scallions, chopped finely 2 tbsp coconut milk
serves 4		2 tbsp soy sauce 1 tbsp sesame oil	4 pork steaks
5 minutes + 1 hour to marinate		1 tbsp lime juice 2 lemongrass stalks, outer leaves removed, chopped finely	lime wedges, to garnish TO SERVE salad stir-fried vegetables
10 minutes			

To make the marinade, place the garlic, pepper, sugar, fish sauce, soy sauce, sesame oil, lime juice, lemongrass, scallions and coconut milk in a large shallow dish and mix well to combine.

Turn the pork steaks in the marinade, then cover the dish with plastic wrap and place in the refrigerator for 1 hour.

Broil the pork steaks under a preheated broiler or barbecue them over charcoal, for 5 minutes on each side, or until cooked through. Garnish with lime wedges and serve with salad or stir-fried vegetables.

tamarind pork

		ingredients	
very easy			
serves 4	SPICE PASTE	2 tbsp tamarind paste	
	4 shallots, chopped finely	2 tbsp hot water	
	2 garlic cloves, chopped finely		
	1 inch/2.5 cm fresh ginger root,	2 tbsp vegetable oil	
	peeled and chopped finely	1 lb 5 oz/600 g lean pork, cut into	
15 minutes	1 tsp ground coriander	thin strips	
	2 fresh red chiles, seeded and	8 oz/225 g canned bamboo shoots,	
	chopped finely	drained	
	½ tsp ground turmeric		
8–10 minutes	6 blanched almonds, chopped finely	cooked noodles, to serve	

To make the spice paste, place the shallots, garlic, ginger, ground coriander, chiles, turmeric, almonds, tamarind paste, and water in a food processor and blend until smooth.

In a wok or skillet, heat the oil over a high heat. Add the pork and cook for 3 minutes, or until the meat is colored. Then add the spice paste and continue to cook for 2 or 3 more minutes.

Add the bamboo shoots and cook for 2 more minutes, or until the pork is cooked through. Serve with hot noodles.

stir-fried lamb
with mint

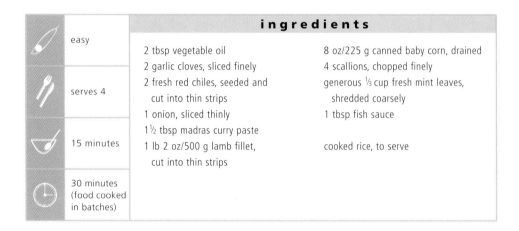

		ingredients	
easy	2 tbsp vegetable oil	8 oz/225 g canned baby corn, drained	
	2 garlic cloves, sliced finely	4 scallions, chopped finely	
serves 4	2 fresh red chiles, seeded and	generous ⅓ cup fresh mint leaves,	
	cut into thin strips	shredded coarsely	
	1 onion, sliced thinly	1 tbsp fish sauce	
15 minutes	1½ tbsp madras curry paste		
	1 lb 2 oz/500 g lamb fillet,	cooked rice, to serve	
	cut into thin strips		
30 minutes (food cooked in batches)			

Heat half the oil in a wok or large skillet. Add the garlic and chile and cook until soft. Remove and set aside. Add the onion and cook for 5 minutes, or until soft. Remove and set aside.

Heat the remaining oil in the wok, then add the curry paste and cook for 1 minute. Add the lamb, in batches if necessary, and cook for 5–8 minutes, or until cooked through and tender.

Return the onion to the wok with the baby corn, scallions, mint, and fish sauce. Cook until heated through. Scatter the garlic and chile over and serve with rice.

stir-fried chicken
with thai basil

		ingredients	
	very easy	2 tbsp vegetable oil	generous ⅓ cup fresh Thai basil
		4 garlic cloves, crushed	leaves, chopped coarsely
	serves 4	4 scallions, chopped finely	2 tbsp fish sauce
		4 green chiles, seeded and	
		chopped finely	basil leaves, to garnish
	15 minutes	1 green bell pepper, seeded and	
		sliced thinly	cooked rice, to serve
		1 lb 5 oz/600 g skinless, boneless	
	15 minutes	chicken breast fillets, cut into	
		thin strips	

Heat the oil in a wok. Add the garlic and scallions and cook for 1–2 minutes, or until soft.

Add the chile peppers and green bell pepper and cook for 2 minutes.

Add the chicken and cook until browned. Stir in the basil and fish sauce, and cook for a few more minutes, or until the chicken is cooked through. Garnish with basil leaves and serve with rice.

quick green
chicken curry

		ingredients
extremely easy		1 tbsp vegetable oil 6 scallions, sliced 1 lb 5oz/600 g skinless, boneless chicken breast, cut into cubes scant 1 cup coconut cream 3 tbsp green Thai curry paste 3 tbsp chopped fresh cilantro
serves 4		
5 minutes		cooked noodles or rice, to serve
10 minutes		

Heat the oil in a large skillet. Add the scallions and the chicken and cook, stirring, for 3–4 minutes, or until the chicken is browned.

Stir in the coconut cream and curry paste and cook for another 5 minutes, or until the chicken is cooked through. Add a little water or bouillon if the sauce becomes too thick.

Stir in the chopped cilantro and serve with rice or noodles.

chicken with
lemongrass & chile

		ingredients	
very easy	2 tbsp vegetable oil	8 chicken thighs with bones and skin
	4 garlic cloves, sliced thinly	3 tbsp fish sauce
serves 4	1 onion, sliced thinly	1 tbsp light brown sugar
	2 lemongrass stalks, outer part removed, chopped very finely	1 cup chicken bouillon
10 minutes	2 red chiles, deseeded and chopped finely	
50 minutes		

Heat the oil in a large skillet. Add the garlic and onion and cook gently for 5–10 minutes, or until soft.

Add the lemongrass and chile and cook for 2 minutes. Add the chicken and cook for 5 minutes, or until browned all over.

Add the fish sauce, sugar, and bouillon. Bring to a boil, then reduce the heat and simmer, covered, for 30 minutes, or until the chicken is cooked through and tender. Stir occasionally and add water, if necessary. Serve immediately.

peanut crusted chicken with dipping sauce

		ingredients	
	easy	2 garlic cloves, crushed	DIPPING SAUCE
		1 inch/2.5 cm fresh root ginger,	1 fresh red chile, seeded
	serves 6	peeled and grated finely	and chopped finely
		1 lemongrass stalk, outer leaves	2 garlic cloves, crushed
		removed, chopped finely	$\frac{1}{2}$ cup white wine vinegar
		2 tbsp chopped fresh cilantro leaves	2 tbsp dark brown sugar
	20 minutes	scant $1\frac{1}{3}$ cups salted peanuts	
		$\frac{3}{4}$ cup all-purpose flour	
		2 eggs	
	35 minutes	4 tbsp milk	
		12 chicken drumsticks, skin removed	

Preheat the oven to 425°F/220°C. Place the garlic, ginger, lemongrass, cilantro leaves, peanuts, and 2 tablespoons of the flour in a food processor and blend until finely ground. Transfer to a shallow dish.

In a bowl, beat together the eggs and milk. Spread the remaining flour on a plate. Dip the drumsticks into the flour, then into the egg mixture and finally into the peanut mixture. Arrange them in an oiled roasting pan. Bake in the oven for 15 minutes, then turn them and cook for another 15 minutes. Pour off any excess oil and cook the drumsticks for 5 more minutes, or until very crisp.

To make the sauce, grind the chile and garlic to a paste using a mortar and pestle. Put the vinegar and sugar in a pan. Heat gently until the sugar dissolves. Bring to a boil and simmer for 2 minutes. Stir in the chile garlic paste. Transfer to a bowl. Drain the drumsticks on paper towels and serve with the sauce.

roast duck salad

		ingredients
very easy		

very easy

serves 4

20 minutes

20–30 minutes

2 duck breasts
2 Boston lettuces, shredded
1 cup beansprouts
1 yellow bell pepper, seeded
   and cut into thin strips
½ cucumber, seeded and
   cut into short thin sticks

GARNISH
2 tsp shredded lime zest
2 tbsp shredded coconut, toasted

DRESSING
juice of 2 limes
3 tbsp fish sauce
1 tbsp soft brown sugar
2 tsp sweet chili sauce
1 inch/2.5 cm fresh root ginger,
   grated finely
3 tbsp chopped fresh mint
3 tbsp chopped fresh basil

Preheat the oven to 400°F/200°C. Place the duck breasts on a rack set over a roasting pan and roast in the oven for 20–30 minutes, or until cooked as desired and the skin is crisp. Remove from the oven and set aside to cool.

In a large bowl, combine the lettuce, beansprouts, bell pepper and cucumber. Cut the cooled duck into strips and add to the salad. Mix well.

In a bowl, whisk together the lime juice, fish sauce, sugar, chili sauce, ginger, mint, and basil. Add the dressing to the salad and toss well.

Turn the salad out onto a serving platter and garnish with the lime zest and shredded coconut before serving.

vegetables, salads, noodles & rice

The vegetable dishes in this section, such as Stir-fried Green Vegetables, can be served as an accompaniment to the main course, or you could serve one or two of the dishes with noodles or rice as a light lunch or supper. If you omit the fish sauce, they are suitable for vegetarians. Rice is the staple food of Thailand, and plain cooked fragrant rice is served at every meal. Spicy Fried Rice is a good accompaniment to a plain main course or can be served as a dish in its own right. Noodles can be combined with a wide variety of different ingredients and are equally good served hot or cold.

stir-fried
green vegetables

		ingredients
extremely easy		

ingredients

2 tbsp vegetable oil
3 garlic cloves, sliced thinly
1 inch/2.5 cm fresh root ginger,
   sliced thinly
6 oz/175 g baby spinach leaves,
   washed and drained
1 small head broccoli,
   cut into small florets
4 oz/115 g green beans, trimmed
   and halved

1 cup snow peas, trimmed
   and halved
freshly ground black pepper
1 tbsp fish sauce
1 tbsp oyster sauce
1 tsp sugar
4 scallions, chopped diagonally

extremely easy

serves 4

15 minutes

10 minutes

Heat the oil in a wok. Cook the garlic and ginger for 1 minute, then add the spinach, broccoli, and beans and cook for 2 minutes.

Add the snow peas and cook all the vegetables over a high heat, for 2 minutes.

Add the pepper, fish sauce, oyster sauce, sugar, and scallions and continue to cook for another 2 minutes.

Transfer to a heated serving plate and serve at once.

vegetable & coconut curry

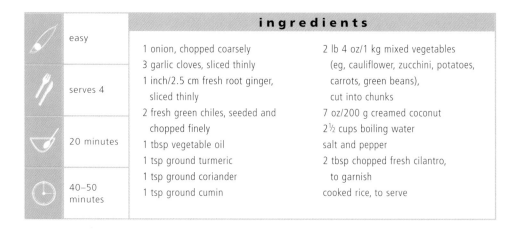

		ingredients
easy		

serves 4	1 onion, chopped coarsely
	3 garlic cloves, sliced thinly
	1 inch/2.5 cm fresh root ginger,
	  sliced thinly
	2 fresh green chiles, seeded and
	  chopped finely
	1 tbsp vegetable oil
	1 tsp ground turmeric
	1 tsp ground coriander
	1 tsp ground cumin
		2 lb 4 oz/1 kg mixed vegetables
		  (eg, cauliflower, zucchini, potatoes,
		  carrots, green beans),
		  cut into chunks
		7 oz/200 g creamed coconut
		2½ cups boiling water
		salt and pepper
		2 tbsp chopped fresh cilantro,
		  to garnish
		cooked rice, to serve

20 minutes		
40–50 minutes		

Put the onion, garlic, ginger, and chiles in a food processor and blend until almost smooth.

Heat the oil in a large pan, then add the onion mixture and cook gently for 5 minutes, stirring constantly.

Add the turmeric, coriander, and cumin and cook for 3–4 minutes, stirring. Add the vegetables and stir to coat in the spice paste.

In a pitcher, mix together the creamed coconut and boiling water and stir until dissolved. Add this coconut milk to the vegetables, then cover and simmer for 30–40 minutes, or until the vegetables are tender.

Season with salt and pepper, then garnish with the chopped cilantro and serve with rice.

thai salad
with peanut dressing

easy	
serves 4	
15 minutes	
10 minutes	

ingredients

2¼ cups white cabbage, shredded
4 carrots, cut into short thin sticks
4 celery stalks, cut into short
   thin sticks
2¼ cups beansprouts
½ cucumber, cut into short thin sticks

PEANUT SAUCE
2 tbsp smooth peanut butter
scant 1 cup coconut cream
2 tsp red Thai curry paste
1 tbsp fish sauce
1 tbsp soft brown sugar

GARNISH
fried onion
sliced green chile

In a steamer set above a pan of boiling water, steam the cabbage, carrots, and celery for 3–4 minutes, or until just tender. Let cool.

Arrange the beansprouts on a large shallow serving dish. Arrange the cabbage, carrots, celery, and cucumber on top.

To make the sauce, place the peanut butter, coconut cream, red Thai curry paste, fish sauce, and sugar in a pan. Heat gently, stirring, adding a little hot water, if necessary, to make a coating sauce. Spoon a little of the sauce over the vegetables and then garnish with fried onions and sliced chile. Serve the rest of the sauce separately.

green papaya salad

		ingredients	
very easy	2 cups snow peas	GARNISH	
	2 unripe papayas	12 cherry tomatoes, halved	
serves 4–6	DRESSING	2 tbsp chopped peanuts	
	2 garlic cloves, crushed		
	2 fresh red chiles, seeded and	½ head of Chinese leaves, to serve	
15 minutes	chopped finely		
	1 tsp sugar		
	2 tbsp soy sauce		
3 minutes	juice of 1 lime		

Place the snow peas in a pan of boiling salted water. Bring back to a boil and cook for 2 minutes. Drain into a strainer, then refresh with cold water. Cut into short thin sticks and place in a bowl.

Peel the papayas and remove the black seeds. Chop the papayas and place in the bowl with the snow peas. Chill until ready to serve.

In a bowl, mix together the garlic, chiles, sugar, soy sauce, and lime juice. Pour over the papaya salad and mix well.

Arrange the Chinese leaves in a large serving bowl. Put the salad on top and garnish with the halved tomatoes and chopped peanuts before serving.

pineapple
& cucumber salad

very easy	
serves 4	
20 minutes	

ingredients

1 cucumber	DRESSING
1 small fresh pineapple	3 tbsp lemon juice
1 red onion, sliced thinly	2 tbsp soy sauce
1 bunch watercress	1 tsp sugar
	1 tsp chile sauce
	2 tbsp chopped fresh mint

Peel the cucumber and cut into fourths lengthwise. Scoop out the seeds with a teaspoon and cut each fourth into ½ inch/1 cm pieces. Place in a bowl.

Peel the pineapple and cut into fourths, lengthwise. Remove the core. Cut each fourth in half lengthwise and cut into ½ inch/1 cm pieces and add to the cucumber. Add the onion and watercress and mix.

To make the dressing, place the lemon juice, soy sauce, sugar, chile sauce, and mint in a bowl and whisk together.

Pour the dressing over the salad and toss together. Transfer to a large serving platter and serve at once.

noodles with shrimp
& green bell peppers

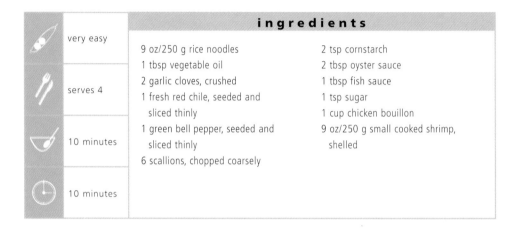

very easy	
serves 4	
10 minutes	
10 minutes	

ingredients

9 oz/250 g rice noodles
1 tbsp vegetable oil
2 garlic cloves, crushed
1 fresh red chile, seeded and
  sliced thinly
1 green bell pepper, seeded and
  sliced thinly
6 scallions, chopped coarsely

2 tsp cornstarch
2 tbsp oyster sauce
1 tbsp fish sauce
1 tsp sugar
1 cup chicken bouillon
9 oz/250 g small cooked shrimp,
  shelled

Prepare the noodles as directed on the packet. Drain, then refresh under cold water and drain again.

Heat the oil in a wok. Add the garlic, chile, bell pepper, and scallions. Cook for 1 minute, then remove from the wok to a plate and set aside.

Blend the cornstarch with a little water and add to the wok with the oyster sauce, fish sauce, sugar, and bouillon. Stir over a medium heat until the mixture boils and thickens.

Return the bell pepper and scallion mixture to the wok with the shrimp and noodles. Cook, stirring, for 2 minutes, or until heated through. Transfer to a heated serving bowl and serve.

fried egg noodles

extremely easy	
serves 4	
10 minutes	
10 minutes	

ingredients

9 oz/250 g fine egg noodles
2 tbsp vegetable oil
2 garlic cloves, crushed
1 tbsp fish sauce
3 tbsp lime juice
1 tsp sugar
2 eggs, beaten lightly
4 oz/115 g cooked shrimp, shelled
1 cup beansprouts
6 scallions, sliced finely

GARNISH
2 tbsp finely chopped roasted peanuts
handful of cilantro leaves
lime slices

Prepare the noodles as directed on the packet. Drain, then rinse with cold water and drain again. Set aside.

Heat the oil in a wok. Add the garlic and cook, stirring, for 1 minute, or until lightly browned but not burned. Stir in the fish sauce, lime juice, and sugar and stir until the sugar has dissolved.

Quickly stir in the eggs and cook for a few seconds. Stir in the noodles to coat with the garlic and eggs. Add the shrimp, beansprouts, and half the scallions.

When everything is heated through, transfer the mixture to a warmed serving dish. Sprinkle the remaining scallions on top and serve, garnished with peanuts, cilantro leaves, and lime slices.

hot & sour
noodle salad

		ingredients	
extremely easy		12 oz/350 g rice vermicelli	1 tsp sugar
		4 tbsp sesame oil	4 scallions, sliced finely
serves 4		3 tbsp soy sauce	1–2 tsp hot chili sauce
		juice of 2 limes	2 tbsp chopped fresh cilantro
5 minutes			
5 minutes			

Prepare the vermicelli as directed on the packet. Drain, then place in a bowl and toss with half the sesame oil.

In a bowl, mix together the remaining oil, the soy sauce, lime juice, sugar, scallions and chili sauce. Stir into the noodles.

Stir in the cilantro and serve.

spicy fried rice

easy

serves 4–6

15 minutes
+ 20 minutes
to soak
mushrooms

25 minutes

ingredients

1¼ cups long grain rice
scant ½ cup dried mushrooms
2 tbsp vegetable oil
2 eggs, beaten lightly
2 garlic cloves, chopped finely
1 fresh red chile, seeded
  and chopped finely
½ inch/1 cm fresh root ginger,
  grated finely

2 tbsp soy sauce
1 tsp sugar
2 tsp fish sauce
6 scallions, chopped finely
1 lb/450 g cooked, shelled
  small shrimp
14 oz/400 g canned baby corn,
  drained and cut in half
3 tbsp chopped fresh cilantro

Place the rice in a strainer and rinse under cold water. Drain thoroughly. Add the rice to a large pan of boiling salted water, then bring back to a boil and cook for about 10 minutes, or until tender. Drain, then rinse under cold water and drain again.

Place the mushrooms in a bowl, cover with warm water and let stand for 20 minutes. Drain and cut into slices.

Heat half the oil in a wok. Add the eggs. Stir the uncooked egg to the outside edge of the wok. Cook until firm. Remove the omelet, then roll up firmly and cut into strips.

Heat the remaining oil in the wok, then add the garlic, chile and ginger and cook for 1 minute. Add the soy sauce, sugar, fish sauce, and scallions, stirring to dissolve the sugar. Stir in the reserved rice, shrimp, and corn, tossing to mix. Cook for 3–4 minutes, or until the rice is heated through. Stir in the cilantro, then turn into a warm serving bowl and serve at once.

desserts

Desserts other than fresh fruit are not
usually served at a Thai meal, but are more
likely to appear at banquets and festive
occasions. The dishes in this section are
delicious at any time, whether served after
dinner or as a snack at another time of day.
These desserts are all light, and most
include fruit. Tropical Fruit in a Lemon
Grass Syrup is fragrant and refreshing at
the end of a meal. Coconut milk or cream
are widely used in the savory recipes in this
book, but they also make creamy desserts
such as the Coconut & Ginger Ice Cream
and Coconut Cream Custard.

mango with sticky rice

		ingredients	
very easy	generous 1 cup glutinous rice, soaked for 30 minutes in cold water	2 tbsp superfine sugar
serves 4	1 cup coconut milk	pinch of salt
30 minutes + 30 minutes to soak rice		2 large ripe mangoes
35 minutes		

Drain the rice and rinse thoroughly. Place in a pan with the coconut milk, sugar, and salt. Bring to a boil and simmer, stirring occasionally, until the rice has absorbed all the coconut milk and is very soft.

Transfer the rice to a steamer set over a pan of simmering water. Cover and steam for 15 minutes. Let cool a little. Spread the rice out on a cookie sheet lined with foil, then roll the rice flat with a wet rolling pin. Cut into diamond shapes.

Peel the mangoes and cut the flesh into cubes. Arrange the rice diamonds and mango cubes on individual plates or in ramekins and serve.

coconut cream custard

		ingredients
extremely easy		4 large eggs
		generous ½ cup superfine sugar
serves 4		scant 1 cup coconut cream
		1 tbsp rosewater
10 minutes		fresh fruit, to serve
20–30 minutes		

Preheat the oven to 350°F/180°C.

In a bowl, beat together the eggs, sugar, coconut cream, and rosewater and stir until the sugar is dissolved.

Divide the custard into four ramekins. Place in a roasting pan and pour in boiling water to come halfway up the sides of the ramekins. Bake in the oven for 20–30 minutes, or until set. Remove from the tin and let cool.

To turn out, run a sharp knife round the edge of each custard and turn out onto a serving dish. Serve with fresh fruit.

tropical fruit
in lemongrass syrup

		ingredients	
easy			
serves 4	LEMONGRASS SYRUP	1 honeydew melon	
	1½ cups superfine sugar	1 small pineapple	
	⅔ cup water	1 papaya	
	2 lemongrass stalks, bruised	14 oz/400 g lychees, pitted	
	2 kaffir lime leaves	3 passion fruit	
15 minutes + 12 hours to chill	juice of 1 lime		
		DECORATION	
		1 tbsp lime zest	
15 minutes		small handful of fresh mint leaves	

To make the syrup, place the sugar, water, lemongrass, and lime leaves and lime juice in a pan. Heat gently until the sugar has dissolved. Bring to a boil and boil, uncovered, for 5 minutes. Set aside overnight.

Cut the melon in half, then remove the seeds and scoop out the flesh with a melon baller. Place in a bowl. Peel the pineapple, then cut into fourths lengthwise and remove the core. Cut into cubes and add to the melon. Peel the papaya, then remove the seeds and cut the flesh into cubes and add to the other fruit.

Add the lychees. Cut the passion fruit in half and scoop the pulp and seeds into the bowl of fruit. Stir to combine, then transfer to a serving bowl. Remove the lemongrass and lime leaves from the syrup and pour over the fruit. Decorate with the lime zest and mint leaves and serve.

thai crêpes with papaya & passion fruit

		ingredients	
easy			
serves 4	2 eggs	FILLING	
	½ cup coconut milk	2 papaya	
	¾ cup milk	3 passion fruit	
15 minutes	1 cup all-purpose flour	juice of 1 lime	
	½ tsp salt	2 tbsp confectioners' sugar	
	1 tbsp superfine sugar		
20 minutes	1 tbsp butter, melted		
	oil, for frying		
	sifted confectioners' sugar, for dusting		

In a bowl, whisk together the eggs, coconut milk, and milk. Sift the flour and salt into a large bowl. Stir in the sugar. Make a well in the middle of the flour and gradually beat in the egg mixture to form a smooth batter. Stir in the melted butter.

Heat an 8–9 inch/20–22.5 cm non-stick skillet and brush with oil. Pour in enough batter to coat the bottom of the skillet. Tip the skillet as you pour it in, so the bottom is evenly coated. Cook until browned on the underside and set on top, then turn the crêpe over and cook the other side. Place on a plate, then cover with foil and keep warm while making the remaining crêpes.

Peel the papaya and halve, then scoop out the seeds, reserving a few. Cut into chunks and place in a bowl. Cut the passion fruit in half. Scoop the seeds and pulp into the bowl. Stir in the lime juice and confectioners' sugar. Put a little filling on one fourth of each crêpe. Fold in half and then into fourths. Dust with sifted confectioners' sugar. Scatter on the reserved papaya seeds serve.

thai bananas

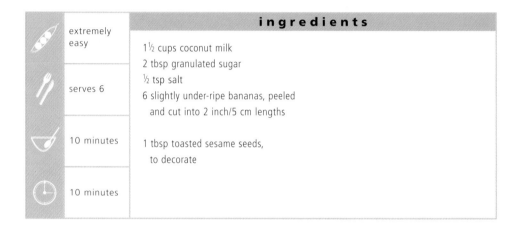

extremely easy	**ingredients**
	1½ cups coconut milk
	2 tbsp granulated sugar
serves 6	½ tsp salt
	6 slightly under-ripe bananas, peeled
	and cut into 2 inch/5 cm lengths
10 minutes	1 tbsp toasted sesame seeds,
	to decorate
10 minutes	

Place the coconut milk, sugar, and salt in a pan and heat gently until the sugar is dissolved. Add the banana pieces and cook gently for 5 minutes, or until the bananas are soft but not mushy.

Divide the mixture between 6 small bowls. Scatter the sesame seeds over and serve.

coconut & ginger
ice cream

very easy	
makes about 1½ pints or 1 litre	
20 minutes + 6–8 hours to freeze	
10 minutes	

ingredients

1¾ cups coconut milk
1 cup whipping cream
4 egg yolks
5 tbsp superfine sugar
4 tbsp syrup from the stem ginger
6 pieces preserved stem ginger, drained and finely chopped
2 tbsp lime juice

TO SERVE
lychees
ginger syrup

Place the coconut milk and cream in a medium pan. Heat gently until just beginning to simmer. Remove from the heat.

In a large bowl, beat together the egg yolks, sugar, and ginger syrup until pale and creamy. Slowly pour in the hot milk mixture, while stirring. Return to the pan and heat gently, stirring constantly, until the mixture thickens and coats the back of a spoon. Remove from the heat and let cool. Stir in the ginger and lime juice.

Transfer the mixture to a freezerproof container. Cover and freeze for 2–3 hours, or until just frozen. Spoon into a bowl and mash with a fork or whisk to break down any ice crystals. Return the mixture to the container and freeze for 2 more hours. Mash once more, then freeze for 2–3 hours, or until firm. Remove from the freezer to the refrigerator 20–30 minutes before serving. Serve with lychees and a little ginger syrup drizzled over.

easy mango ice cream

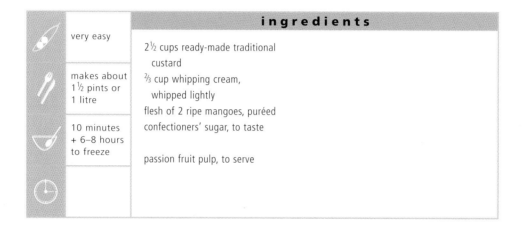

		ingredients
very easy		2½ cups ready-made traditional custard
makes about 1½ pints or 1 litre		⅔ cup whipping cream, whipped lightly
		flesh of 2 ripe mangoes, puréed
10 minutes + 6–8 hours to freeze		confectioners' sugar, to taste
		passion fruit pulp, to serve

In a large bowl, mix together the custard, cream and mango pulp.

Taste for sweetness and, if necessary, add confectioners' sugar to taste, remembering that when frozen, the mixture will taste less sweet.

Transfer the mixture to a freezerproof container. Cover and freeze for 2–3 hours, or until just frozen. Spoon into a bowl and mash with a fork or whisk to break down any ice crystals. Return the mixture to the container and freeze for 2 more hours. Mash once more, then freeze for 2–3 hours, or until firm.

Transfer from the freezer to the refrigerator 20–30 minutes before serving. Serve with the passion fruit pulp.

index